YOUNG ZOOLOGIST

GREEN SEA TURTLE

A FIRST FIELD GUIDE TO THE OCEAN REPTILE FROM THE TROPICS

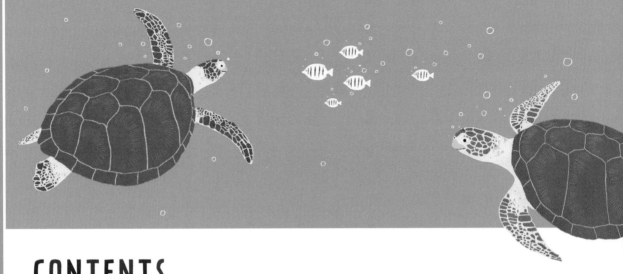

CONTENTS

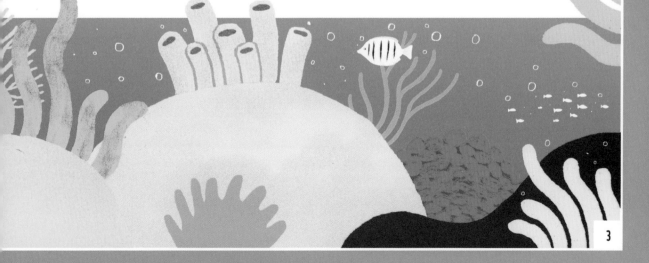

HELLO YOUNG ZOOLOGIST!

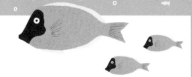

I'm Carlee Jackson, a marine biologist based in Florida. I fell in love with the ocean at a young age. I'm excited to introduce you to one of my favorite animals: the green sea turtle. There are so many cool things to learn about these incredible creatures—for example, the key role they play in keeping our oceans healthy. Unfortunately all species of sea turtle are endangered. That means they need our help. Come with me on a deep dive into the world of green sea turtles, and hopefully you will find them as awesome as I do!

CARLEE JACKSON

FACT FILE

SCIENTIFIC NAME
Chelonia mydas

CLASS
Reptile

FAMILY
Cheloniidae (hard-shelled sea turtles)

LIFE SPAN
60+ years

SIZE COMPARISON

Green sea turtles are the second largest sea turtle.

Kemp's ridley sea turtles are the smallest species.

Leatherback sea turtles are the largest species in the world.

EATS

Seagrass   Algae   Jellyfish

WEIGHT
300–350 lb (135–160 kg)

HABITAT
Tropical oceans

CONSERVATION STATUS
Endangered

5

BEFORE YOU GET STARTED

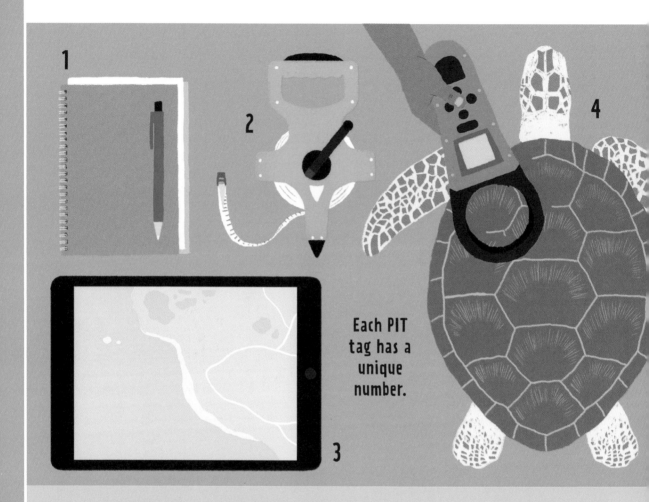

1

2

4

Each PIT tag has a unique number.

3

1 FIELD NOTEBOOK
A waterproof notebook is one of the most important pieces of equipment for a field biologist. It's used to keep track of nesting data and take notes on turtles that may have washed ashore.

2 TAPE MEASURES
Tape measures are used to measure many different things you might come across on the beach. They can be used to measure distances between turtle nests, and the lengths of the turtles themselves.

3 TABLET
A tablet is used to mark where a turtle nest is on a map using GPS (a system that uses satellites to calculate your position on Earth). This helps biologists know the locations of all the sea turtle nests that are on the beach.

A sea turtle biologist can find themselves on the beach at night looking for nesting female sea turtles, or in the early mornings marking sea turtle nests. The weather can be unpredictable. It's important to be prepared, come rain or shine!

Wood stakes

DO NOT DISTURB!

SEA TURTLE NESTING SITE

Mallet

Nest signs tell beachgoers not to touch sea turtle nests.

5

6

Flagging tape

4 **PIT TAG SCANNER**
Sea turtles that are rescued or that wash onto the beach are always checked for PIT tags. Like microchips, they're inserted into sea turtles by scientists or vets to keep track of individual turtles.

5 **NEST-MARKING SUPPLIES**
To mark a sea turtle nest on the beach, you need three wood stakes, flagging tape, a mallet to hammer in the stakes, and a nest sign (for more information, see pages 28–29).

6 **DIGITAL CAMERA**
A field biologist's best friend is a camera! The camera is used to document sea turtle nests or injured turtles. Photos help scientists remember important information about a turtle or its nest.

MEET THE GREEN SEA TURTLE

Green sea turtles are the only plant-eating (herbivore) sea turtle species. Do you know the saying "you are what you eat"? Well, these turtles eat so many plants that they turn green inside! That's where their name comes from.

HOME SWEET HOME

A green sea turtle's shell, or "carapace," is its permanent home. It can't leave its shell or hide inside it. The shell is made of hard scales, called scutes, and it is the turtle's main defense against hungry predators.

SCALY SKIN

The scales on a turtle's skin are different than the ones on its shell. Though not as hard as the shell, these scales also act as a form of protection.

A TALE OF TAILS

The tail is how we can tell females and males apart. Males, like this one, have very long tails that can be up to 1 ft (30 cm) long! Female green sea turtles have short tails.

Green sea turtles can't breathe underwater—but they can hold their breath for up to four hours!

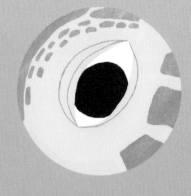

GOOD EYESIGHT

Green sea turtles have large eyes, giving them excellent eyesight underwater in order to search for algae or other plants. They can see many colors, but not orange or red!

SHARP BEAK

With sea grass, algae, and other plants on the menu, green sea turtles need sharp beaks to cut through their food. Their beaks are serrated like a saw.

NOSTRILS

The nostrils, or "nares," are used for smelling. Sea turtles have a very good sense of smell. They pull in water through their nostrils to get a good "sniff" of the water!

POWERFUL FLIPPERS

The front and back flippers play different roles in sea turtle swimming. The front flippers act as the motor, propelling the turtle forward at speeds of up to 22 mph (35 kph). Meanwhile, the back flippers help the turtle change direction.

The Eastern Pacific subspecies of green sea turtle is called the black sea turtle. It is the only sea turtle that is known to come out of the ocean to bask in the sunlight.

THE FAMILY

LEATHERBACK

As the largest species of sea turtle, leatherbacks can weigh up to 2,000 lb (900 kg)! They get their name from their have soft, flexible shells. Leatherbacks can dive a mile deep into the ocean, where they feed on jellyfish.

LOGGERHEAD

These turtles can thank their giant heads and strong jaws for their name. Loggerheads are carnivores (meat eaters) and use their strong jaws to crush through the shells of their favorite foods: crabs, lobster, and conches.

Green sea turtles aren't the only sea turtle on the block. In fact, sea turtles are found all over the world! Each species varies in size, diet, and habitat, but they all call the ocean their home.

OLIVE RIDLEY

Olive ridleys have an olive-green shell. They're the most abundant species of sea turtle found in the Atlantic and Pacific oceans. Olive ridleys are omnivorous, meaning they eat both plants (such as algae) and animals (such as crabs).

FLATBACK

Unlike most other turtle species, which travel great distances, flatbacks spend their lives nesting, breeding, and feeding in Australian waters. These animals from Down Under get their name from their flat shells.

There are seven species of sea turtle in the world.

KEMP'S RIDLEY

The smallest and rarest of the sea turtle species, Kemp's ridleys are found in the eastern North Atlantic and the Gulf of Mexico. They're named after the fisherman who first discovered them.

HAWKSBILL

Hawksbills live in tropical coral reefs around the world. They use their birdlike beaks to feed on sea sponges and sea anemones. Hawksbills are very important for the health of coral reef ecosystems.

ALL AROUND THE WORLD

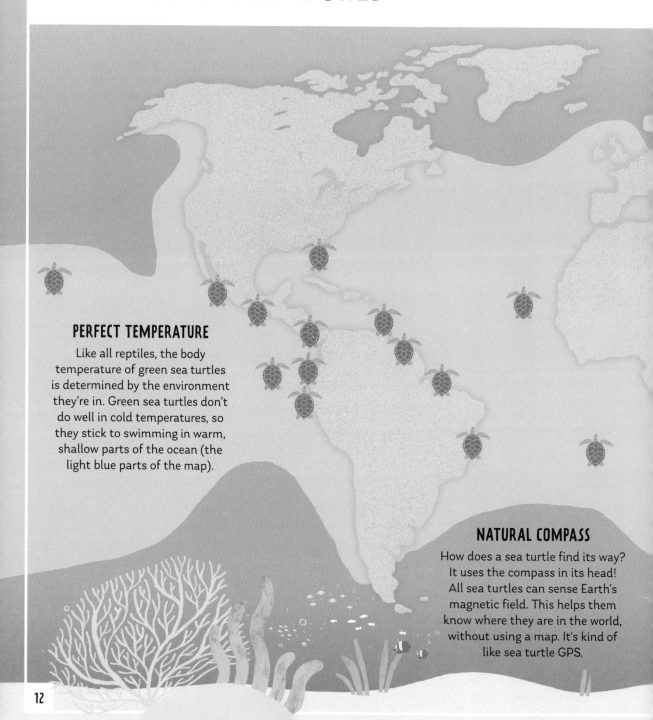

PERFECT TEMPERATURE

Like all reptiles, the body temperature of green sea turtles is determined by the environment they're in. Green sea turtles don't do well in cold temperatures, so they stick to swimming in warm, shallow parts of the ocean (the light blue parts of the map).

NATURAL COMPASS

How does a sea turtle find its way? It uses the compass in its head! All sea turtles can sense Earth's magnetic field. This helps them know where they are in the world, without using a map. It's kind of like sea turtle GPS.

Where there's warm water, you can probably find green sea turtles! They spend time swimming, eating, and nesting across the globe in tropical and subtropical waters. There are worse places to spend your time....

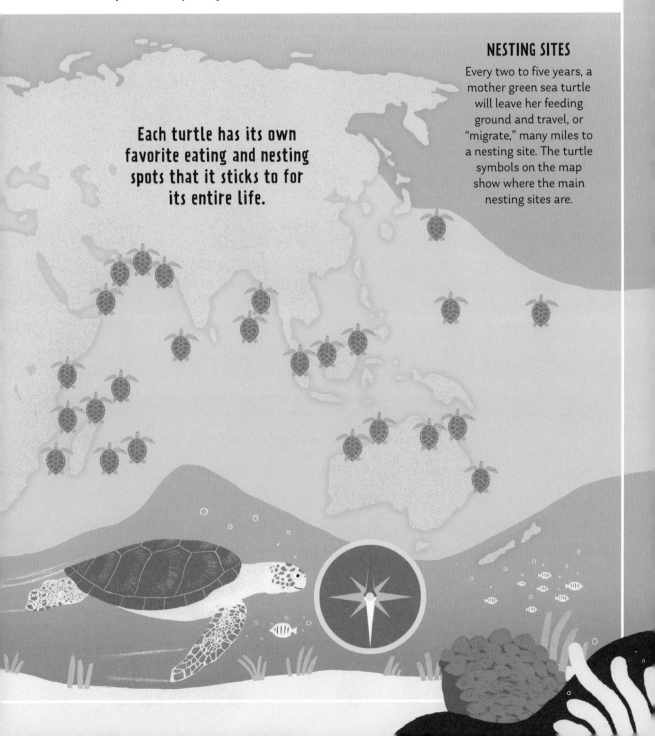

Each turtle has its own favorite eating and nesting spots that it sticks to for its entire life.

NESTING SITES

Every two to five years, a mother green sea turtle will leave her feeding ground and travel, or "migrate," many miles to a nesting site. The turtle symbols on the map show where the main nesting sites are.

SEAGRASS MOWERS

Using their sharp beaks, green sea turtles mow through their favorite food: seagrass. Green sea turtles play a very important role in keeping this important habitat clean and healthy! Without their lawn mowers, seagrass could grow too much, causing problems in the ecosystem.

TURTLE GRASS

Can you guess what a green sea turtle's favorite type of seagrass is? It's called turtle grass! This flat, ribbon-shaped seagrass is found in shallow, sandy areas near the shore.

PROTECTING SEAGRASS

Seagrass habitats are full of marine animals, and they provide food for many different creatures. Lots of baby marine animals also use seagrass habitats as safe places in which to grow up. Seagrasses, like trees, store carbon inside them. Too much carbon in the atmosphere results in climate change, so it is important to protect seagrass beds in order to keep the planet healthy.

Dugongs will only eat seagrass!

ALGAE EATERS

If it's green, it can't escape the beak of a green sea turtle! These reptiles like to munch on algae almost as much as seagrass. Algae grows on things such as rocks—the turtles scrape it off using their beaks.

CARAPACE COMPANIONS

Green sea turtles have interesting relationships with many different sea creatures. Green sea turtles very rarely swim alone! When two different species form a relationship, it is called symbiosis.

FISH BUDDIES

Green sea turtles get along well with cleaner-fish species such as wrasse and doctorfish. Turtles will seek out the fish when too much algae has grown on their shell. The fish get free food, and the turtle leaves with a clean shell! This is called a mutualistic relationship—everyone benefits.

TURTLE TAXI

Fish called remora sometimes get a free ride on a green sea turtle's back. They have a suction pad on their heads (kind of like a bath toy) that they use to attach to moving animals.

Green turtles and remoras are in a commensal relationship. Remoras neither hurt nor provide benefits to the turtle.

PESKY PARASITES

Some companions are not welcomed—parasites. These animals can harm sea turtles. Creatures such as barnacles attach themselves to turtle shells and can be itchy and uncomfortable. Barnacles usually attach themselves to unmoving surfaces, so a sea turtle with many barnacles is not a good sign. It can mean that the turtle hasn't been swimming and could be sick or injured.

Whales can get barnacles on their skin too!

Barnacles can cause dents or bumps on a turtle's shell.

A DAY IN THE LIFE

DINNERTIME

Seagrass really hits the spot! If there is a good patch of seagrass in an area, you can find multiple green sea turtles munching on their seagrass salads until they're full.

SCRATCH THAT ITCH

Who doesn't like a good back scratch? Green sea turtles find rocks or coral to wiggle under for a nice shell scratch. This helps get rid of barnacles!

Eat, sleep, swim, repeat! Green sea turtles are pretty simple when it comes to their daily habits. When they are young or feeding they can be found with other turtles, but most of the time they are swimming solo.

A LONG JOURNEY

Using the compass in their heads, green sea turtles migrate up to 1,250 miles (2,000 km) between their feeding and nesting grounds. They will occasionally swim into a fellow green sea turtle along the way.

NAP TIME

Turtles need their rest. After swimming and eating all day, they will find a rock or patch of coral where they can take a snooze. Green sea turtles can nap up to 11 hours a day.

TIME TO NEST

1 ## SCOUTING A SPOT

First, the female green sea turtle swims along the shore, poking her head above the water to look for a dark, quiet area that will be suitable for her nest.

2 ## CRAWLING

When she sees the ideal area, she crawls out of the ocean and up the beach. She moves both flippers at the same time, leaving a butterfly pattern in the sand behind her.

3 ## GET DIGGING

Once she picks a good spot on the beach, the green sea turtle uses her powerful front flippers to dig herself a deep body pit. She can move up to 2,200 lb (1,000 kg) of sand during this process!

Green sea turtles spend their entire lives in the ocean, except when it's time to nest! Females lay their eggs in the sand on beaches all over the world—but always at the beach where they were born. Nesting happens at night.

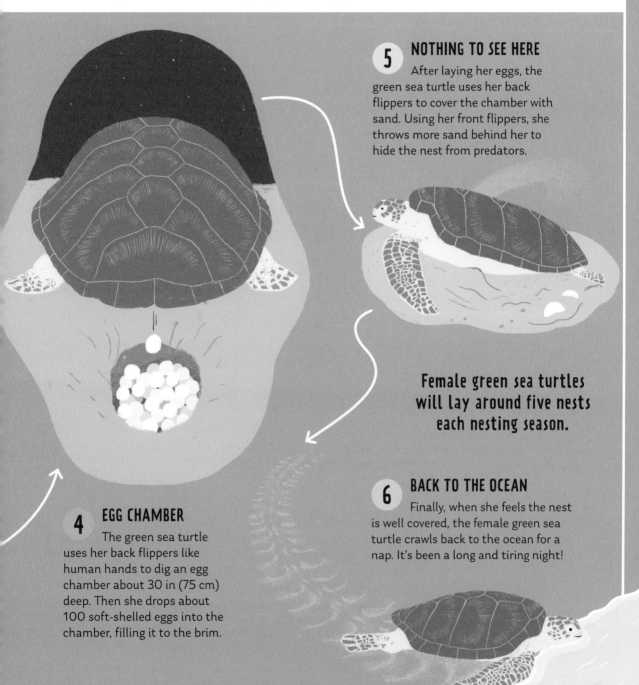

5 NOTHING TO SEE HERE

After laying her eggs, the green sea turtle uses her back flippers to cover the chamber with sand. Using her front flippers, she throws more sand behind her to hide the nest from predators.

Female green sea turtles will lay around five nests each nesting season.

4 EGG CHAMBER

The green sea turtle uses her back flippers like human hands to dig an egg chamber about 30 in (75 cm) deep. Then she drops about 100 soft-shelled eggs into the chamber, filling it to the brim.

6 BACK TO THE OCEAN

Finally, when she feels the nest is well covered, the female green sea turtle crawls back to the ocean for a nap. It's been a long and tiring night!

HATCHING FRENZY

After about two months of staying warm (incubating) in the sand, the green sea turtles begin to hatch from their eggs. They wait until the sun goes down and the sand is cool before climbing out of their nest. A newborn sea turtle is called a hatchling. Hatchlings embark on a long and hazardous journey once they leave the nest.

Hatchlings are about the size of your palm when they are born. They take about 25 years to grow big and strong.

DASHING TO SEA

All the eggs hatch together. It's a big group effort to climb their way out of the sand and onto the beach. The hatchlings then scurry to the ocean as fast as they can, hoping to evade predators along the way.

SMALL BUT MIGHTY

The green sea turtle mothers don't come back to care for their young. But it doesn't matter—hatchlings know how to behave like a green sea turtle from the moment they are born!

FOLLOW THE MOON

The eggs hatch at night. Hatchlings head toward the brightest light source, which is usually the ocean. A full moon can act as a guide, making it easier for hatchlings to find their way to the sea.

SEAWEED BEDS

Once hatchlings reach the ocean, they swim for miles until reaching the protection of floating seaweed beds. They make these floating islands their home for the next few years, eating the small animals that live in the seaweed.

The temperature of the sand determines if a hatchling will be male or female. Hot sand produces females, while cooler sand leads to males!

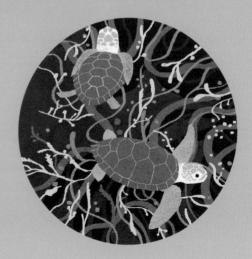

WATCH OUT!

DANGER ON THE BEACH

Animals such as raccoons looking for a yummy snack will sniff out freshly laid green sea turtle nests. If they find one, they will dig it up and feast on the yolk inside the eggs.

ON THE SAND

Birds and crabs wait near the water's edge for hatchlings to come their way. The young green sea turtles have to be lucky to escape these predators.

Herons and ghost crabs pick off hatchlings while they crawl to the water.

From the time eggs are laid in the sand, green sea turtles are high on the menu for many predators. After making it to the ocean, the hatchlings need to eat as much as possible so they can quickly grow and avoid being eaten!

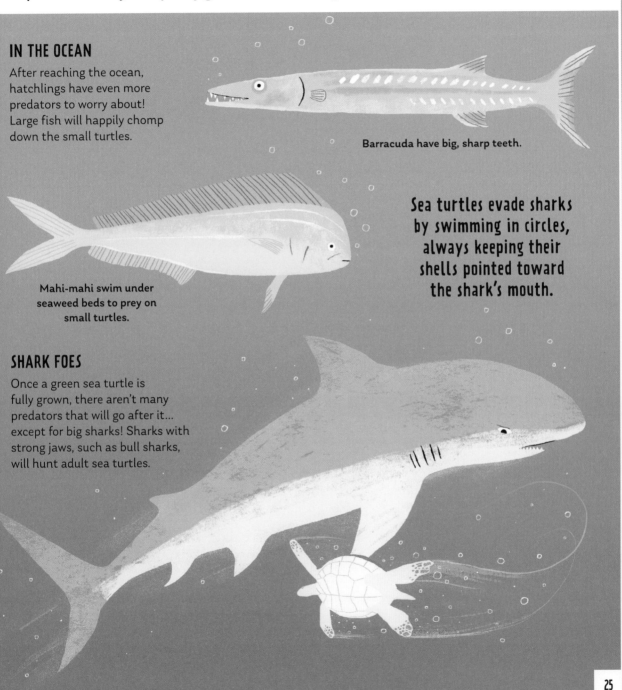

IN THE OCEAN

After reaching the ocean, hatchlings have even more predators to worry about! Large fish will happily chomp down the small turtles.

Barracuda have big, sharp teeth.

Mahi-mahi swim under seaweed beds to prey on small turtles.

Sea turtles evade sharks by swimming in circles, always keeping their shells pointed toward the shark's mouth.

SHARK FOES

Once a green sea turtle is fully grown, there aren't many predators that will go after it... except for big sharks! Sharks with strong jaws, such as bull sharks, will hunt adult sea turtles.

25

TURTLE TROUBLES

Hatchlings attracted to city lights can be run over by cars.

1 BOATS
Green sea turtle shells are no match for boat propellers. When sea turtles come to the surface to breathe, they are at risk of getting hit by boats. It's important to be a responsible boater!

2 FISHING NETS
Abandoned fishing nets floating in the ocean are called ghost nets. Sea turtles can become entangled in these nets while swimming. This makes it hard for them to swim, can damage their flippers, and can be fatal.

3 BRIGHT LIGHTS
Light pollution on beaches makes it harder for nesting or hatchling green sea turtles to find the ocean (see pages 22–23). On beaches near big cities, sea turtles can become confused and crawl the wrong way—away from the ocean.

We've seen that turtles encounter all types of predators starting from the day they are born. But did you know that only about 1 in 10,000 hatchlings will survive to adulthood? On top of predators, sea turtles have another thing to worry about: humans.

4 PLASTIC POLLUTION
Plastic can be found in many different shapes and sizes in the ocean. Green turtles can get entangled and stuck in plastic. It's also common for them to confuse plastic bags for jellyfish and accidentally eat them.

5 CLIMATE CHANGE
Climate change is causing Earth to get hotter. This in turn leads to hotter beach sand, which is a danger to green sea turtle nests. The oceans are also warming, which is changing the migration patterns of turtles.

6 OIL SPILLS
Oil spills from ships cause long-lasting environmental damage and are a danger to green sea turtles. The turtles become ill from swimming among the oil, and their food becomes contaminated.

CONSERVATION

Green sea turtles are sadly endangered, but all around the world conservationists are working hard to protect these precious animals. Scientists, students, vets, park rangers, and volunteers all have important roles to play in helping green sea turtles. Maybe after reading this book you will be inspired to help, too!

NEST MARKING

Conservationists on beaches around the world monitor, document, and mark nests laid by green sea turtles. On beaches where turtles and humans share the same space, marking nests with stakes and a sign protects them from being trampled. Keeping turtle nests safe is an important step in their conservation, and it helps us learn more about how well sea turtle populations are doing.

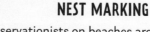

Conservationists mark nests early in the morning after green sea turtles have laid their eggs.

I'VE GOT MY EYE ON YOU

Sometimes scientists attach satellite tags to green sea turtles to learn more about their behavior and movements. This information can help us better understand when and where these turtles go, leading to better conservation.

People are trained on how to mark a green sea turtle nest, so the stakes don't disturb the eggs.

TURTLE HOSPITALS

There are sea turtle hospitals around the world that care for ill and injured sea turtles, with a hope of eventually releasing them back into the ocean. Vets can perform operations on turtles that have swallowed fishing hooks. They can bandage up turtles that have collided with boats.

GLOSSARY

Algae
A large group of aquatic plants with no stems or roots.

Carapace
The top shell of a turtle.

Carnivore
An animal that eats only meat.

Coral reef
An underwater ecosystem made up of lots of living corals (small marine animals).

Ecosystem
A community made up of living things interacting with their environment.

Endangered
A species is endangered, or at risk of going extinct, if its population numbers are very low.

Habitat
An area where an animal or a plant lives.

Hatchling
A newly hatched baby sea turtle that hasn't made its way out to sea yet.

Herbivore
An animal that only eats plants.

Marine biologist
A scientist who studies life in the ocean.

Migration
The seasonal travel of animals from one area to another.

Nares
Another word for nostrils.

Omnivore
An animal that eats both plants and meat.

Parasite
An organism that gets its food by living on or inside another animal, at the cost of the host's health.

PIT tags
A small "microchip" identification tag inserted into an animal so scientists can track its behavior and movement.

Predator
An animal that hunts other animals for its food.

Prey
An animal that is hunted and eaten by predators.

Scutes
The hard scales on a turtle's carapace. This is their main defense against predators.

Symbiosis
The relationship between two different living things, for example a green sea turtle and a doctorfish.

INDEX

This has been a

NEON SQUID

production

Working with sea turtles was my very first job in the marine science field. I'm dedicating this book to Gumbo Limbo and my marine turtle family, my "turtle girls," and all of those who helped further my passion for marine conservation. I'm so grateful to have worked with such amazing animals and humans!

Author: Carlee Jackson
Illustrator: Daniel Rieley

Editorial Assistant: Malu Rocha
US Editor: Allison Singer Kushnir
Proofreader: Laura Gilbert

Copyright © 2023
St. Martin's Press
120 Broadway, New York,
NY 10271

Created for St. Martin's Press
by Neon Squid
The Stables, 4 Crinan Street,
London, N1 9XW

EU representative: Macmillan
Publishers Ireland Ltd,
1st Floor, The Liffey Trust Centre,
117–126 Sheriff Street Upper,
Dublin 1, D01 YC43

10 9 8 7 6 5 4 3 2 1

The right of Carlee Jackson to be identified as the author of this work has been asserted in accordance with the Copyright, Designs and Patents Act, 1988.

Library of Congress Cataloging-in-Publication Data is available.

Printed and bound by
Leo Paper Products Ltd.
Printing in China.

ISBN: 978-1-684-49308-1

Published in June 2023.

www.neonsquidbooks.com